Share your colored versions with us ! We love seeing your results and hearing from you we are social !

The Official FB book page, stay on top of what we have in the works !
www.facebook.com/AMVWART
The Community group, share your colored pages, meet the artists, enjoy exclusive freebies, take part in community Charity books and so much more......
www.facebook.com/groups/fansandfriendsamvwart
www.facebook.com/groups/ColorAWeirdieADay
Follow us on Twitter.... @GlobalDoodlegem
We are on Instagram too
@globaldoodlegems for instagram
...and if you are not social like that we have a blog
globaldoodlegems.wordpress.com

Copyright © 2018 Global Doodle Gems
All rights are reserved by Global Doodle Gems.
Duplication of pages for personal use are allowed. You are invited to color the pages then scan/post your coloured versions to social networks, mentioning the book title and author/artist Maria Wedel (Global DoodleGems).

All artwork and images are protected by copyright laws. This book or any portion thereof may not, otherwise, be reproduced and/or distributed or transmitted without the express written permission of the artist/publisher of Global Doodle Gems.
All of us from the Global Doodle Gems wish you a colortastic time and look forward to seeing your wonderful color results online !

Mini'Weirdies 101 The pages

This collection contains the full pages of all the new Mini'Weirdies that I drew for A Mini'Weirdie A Day and for Mini'Weirdie's Collection volumes 1 to 12.
So in that respect here you get the pages exactly as they were drawn.. cleaned and vectored and uncut.
I hope you will enjoy the collection and have lot's of coloring fun with it !

Kind regards
Maria Wedel

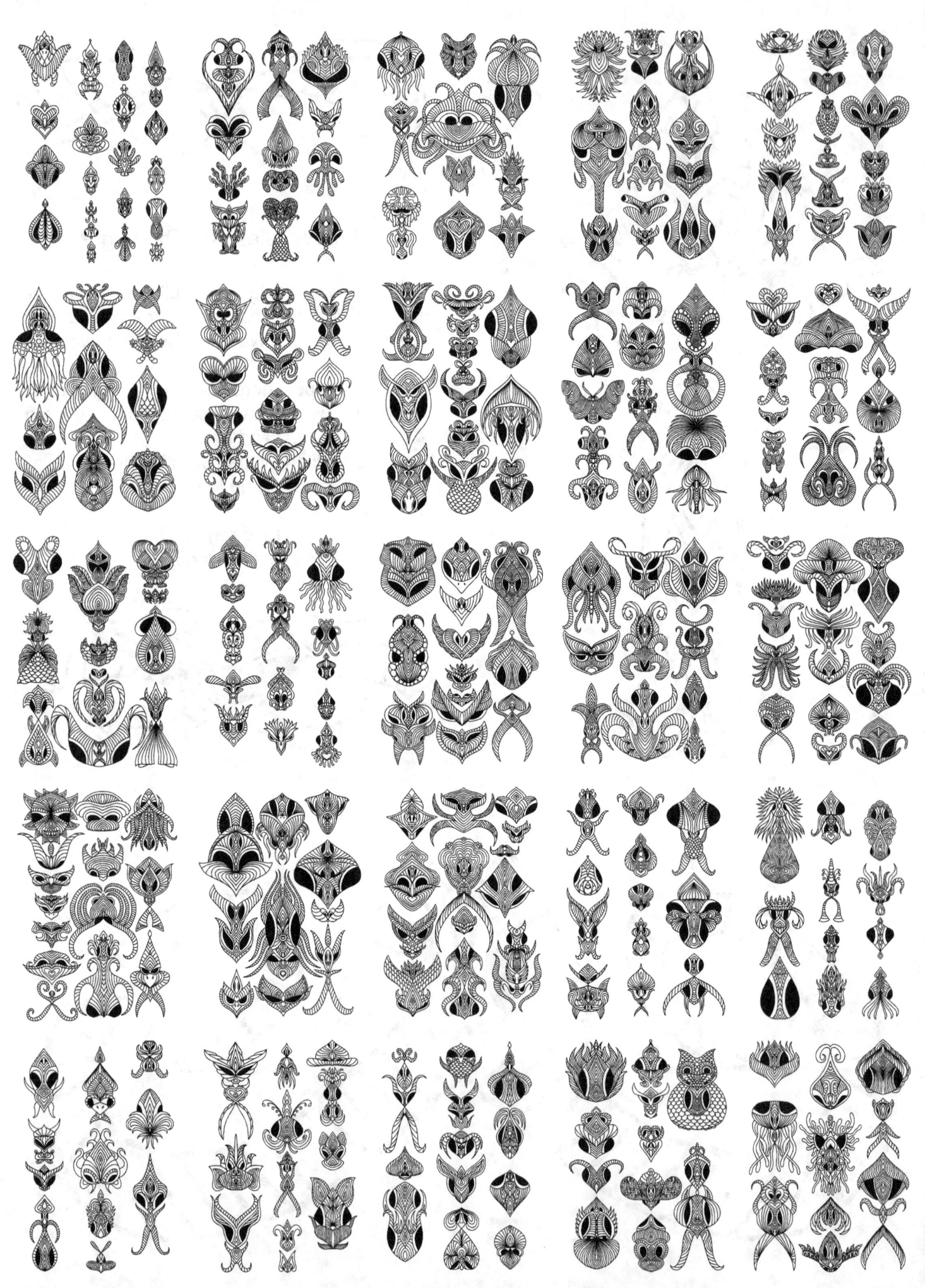

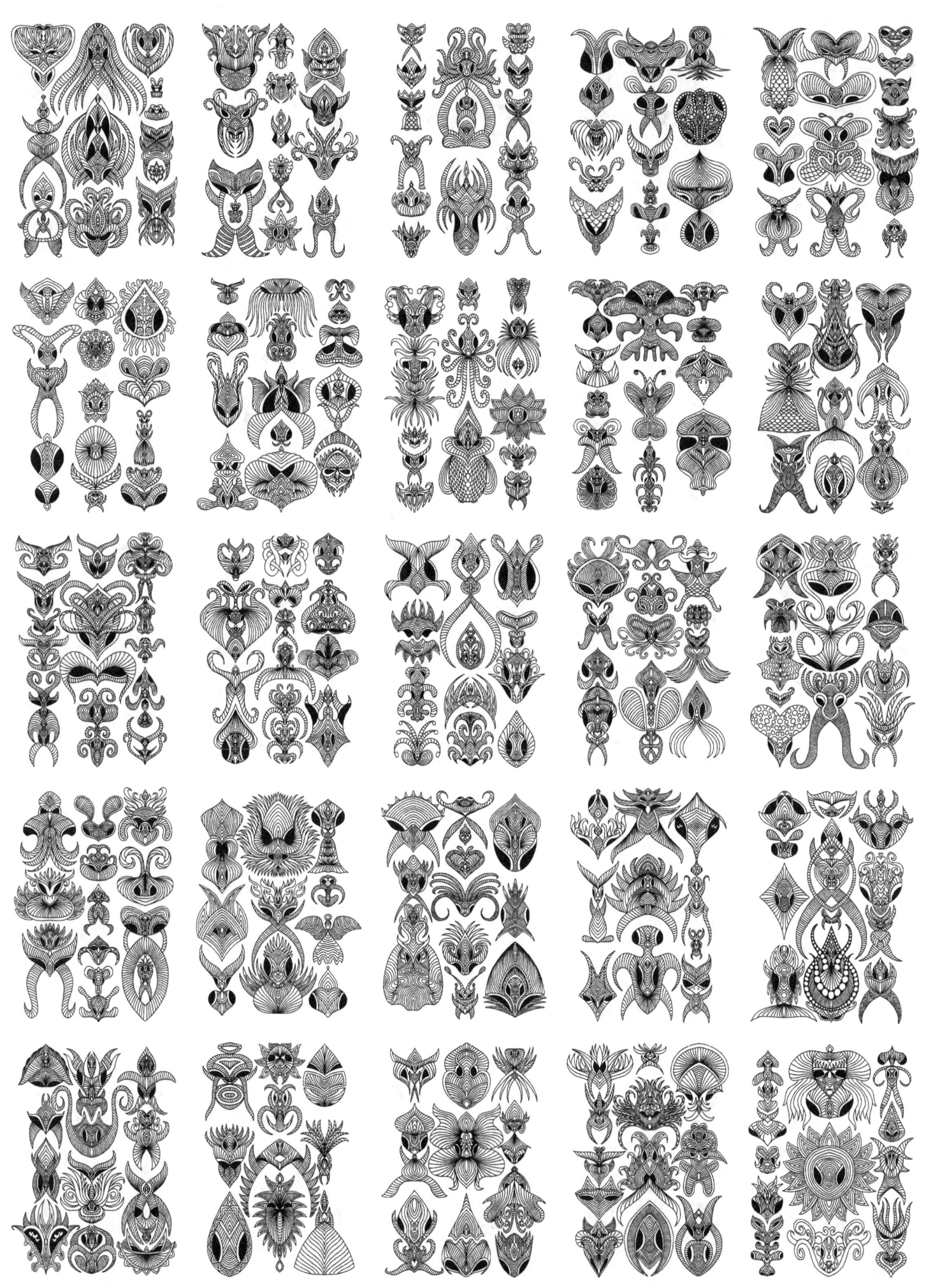

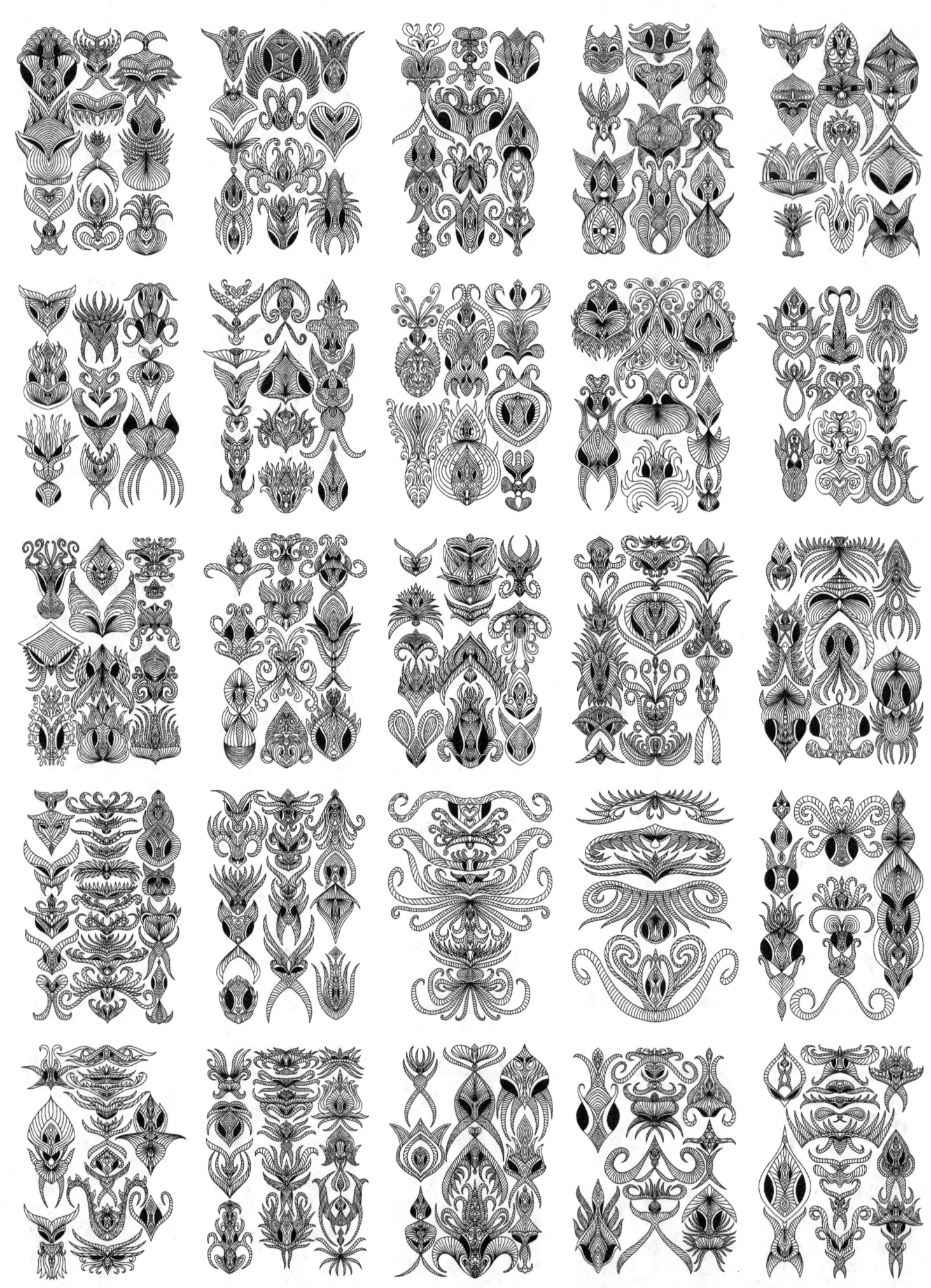

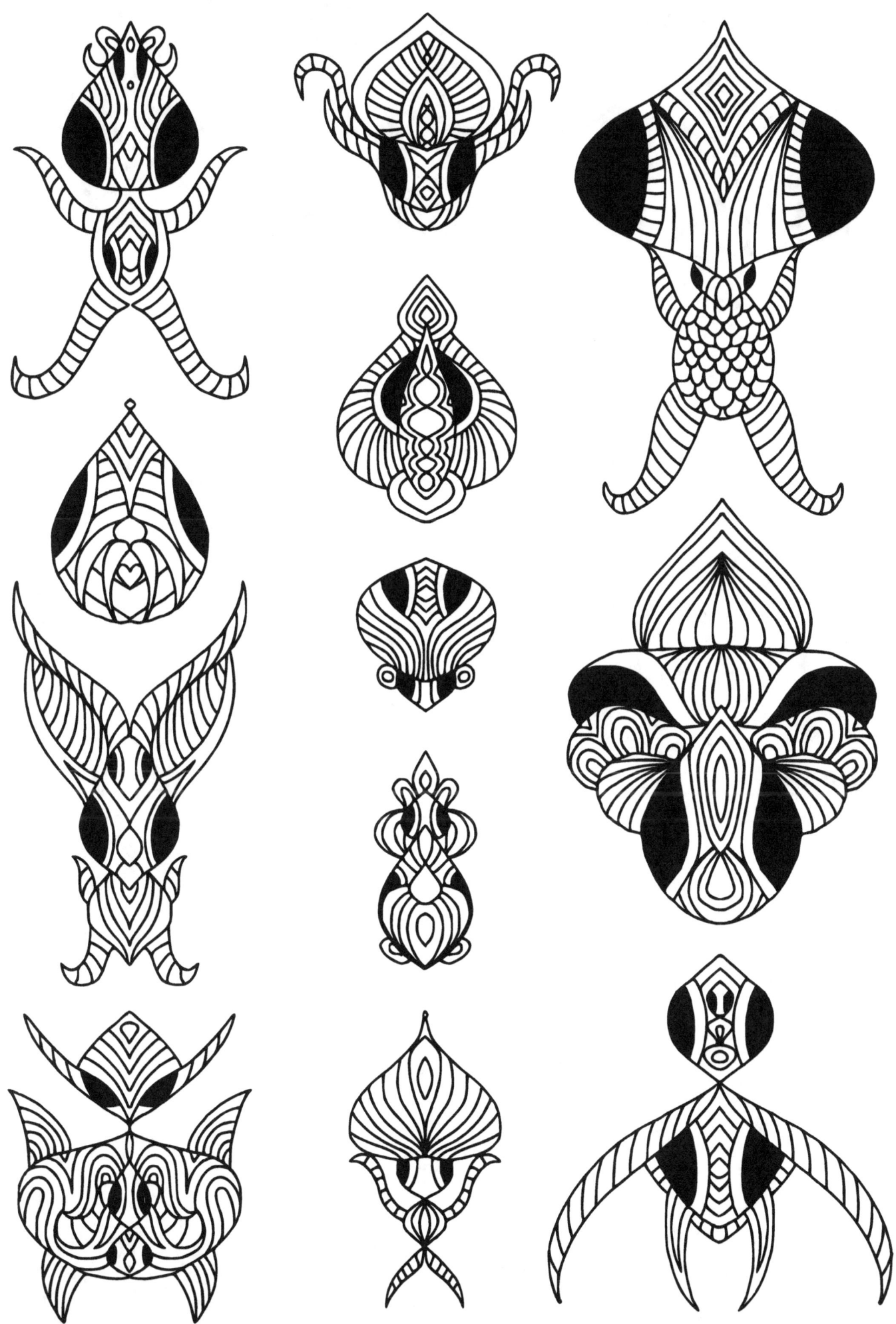

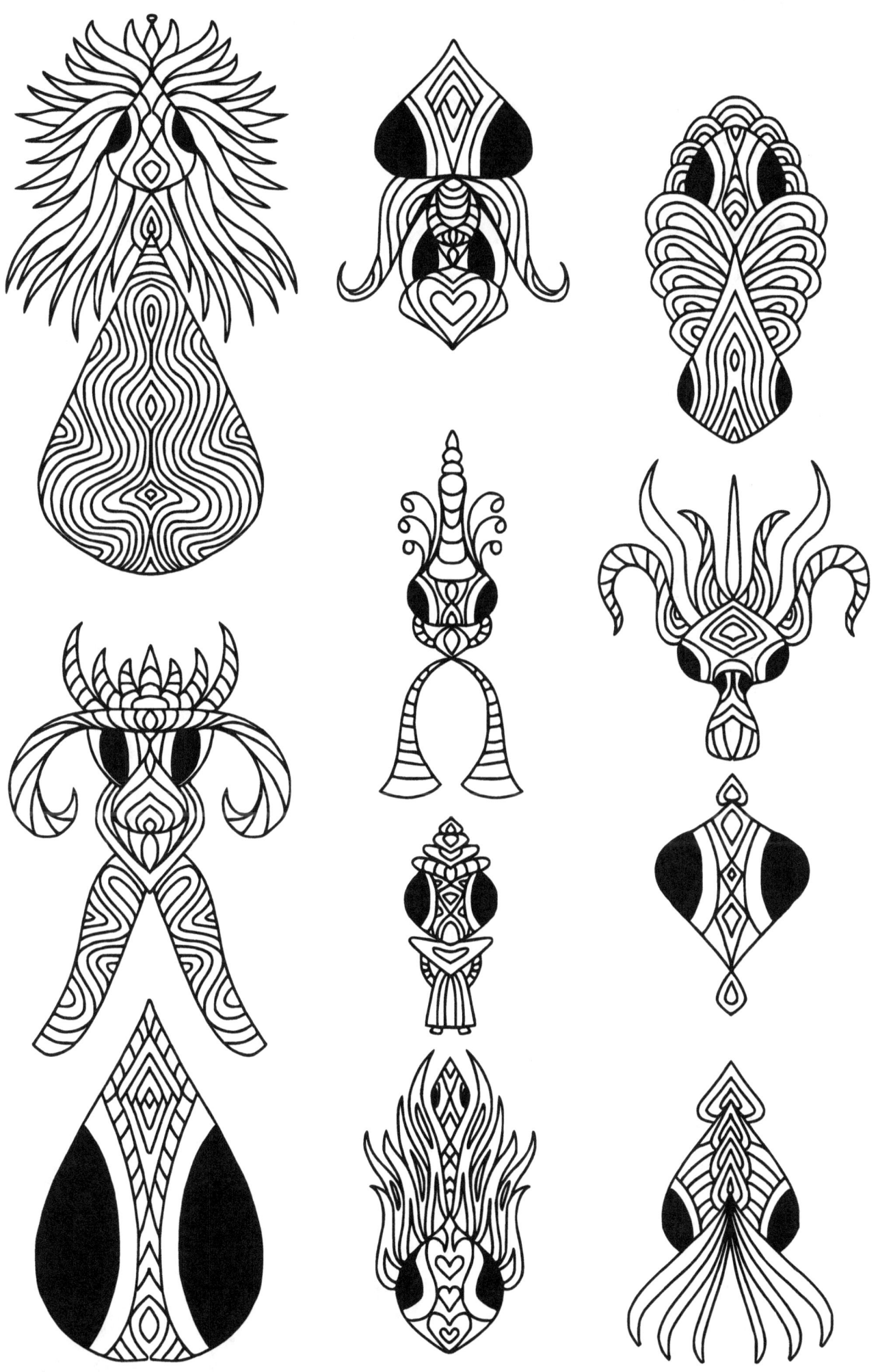

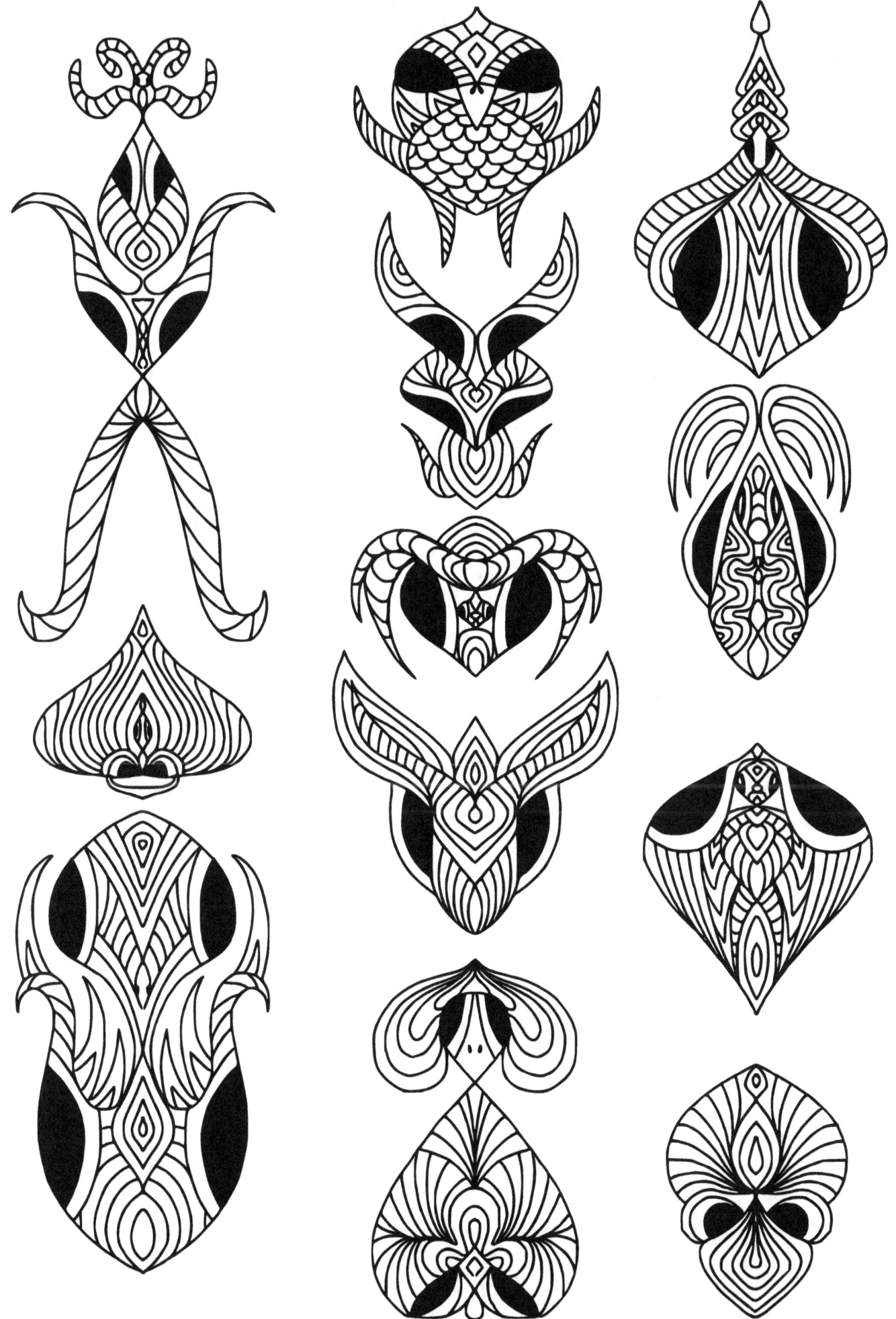

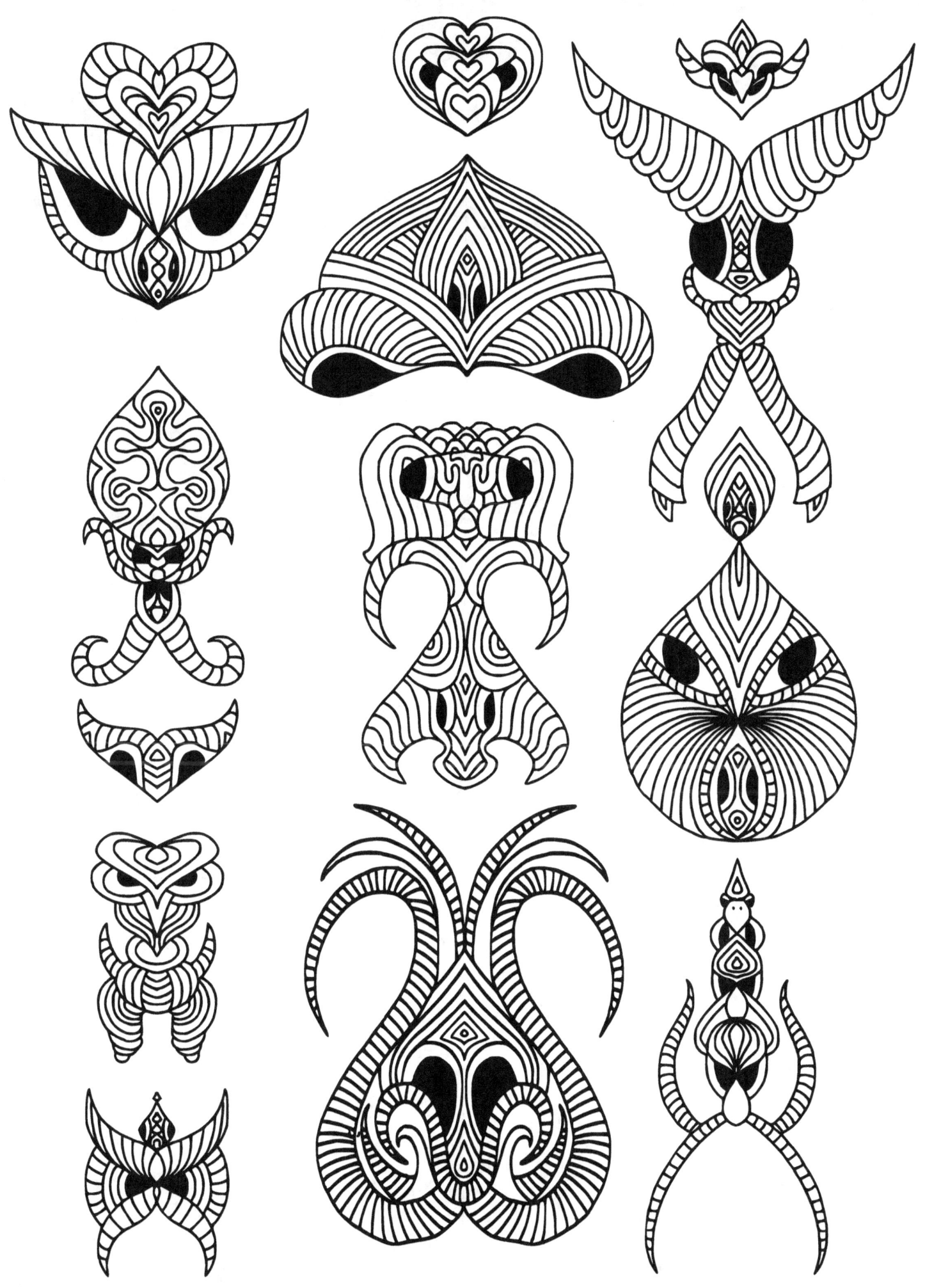

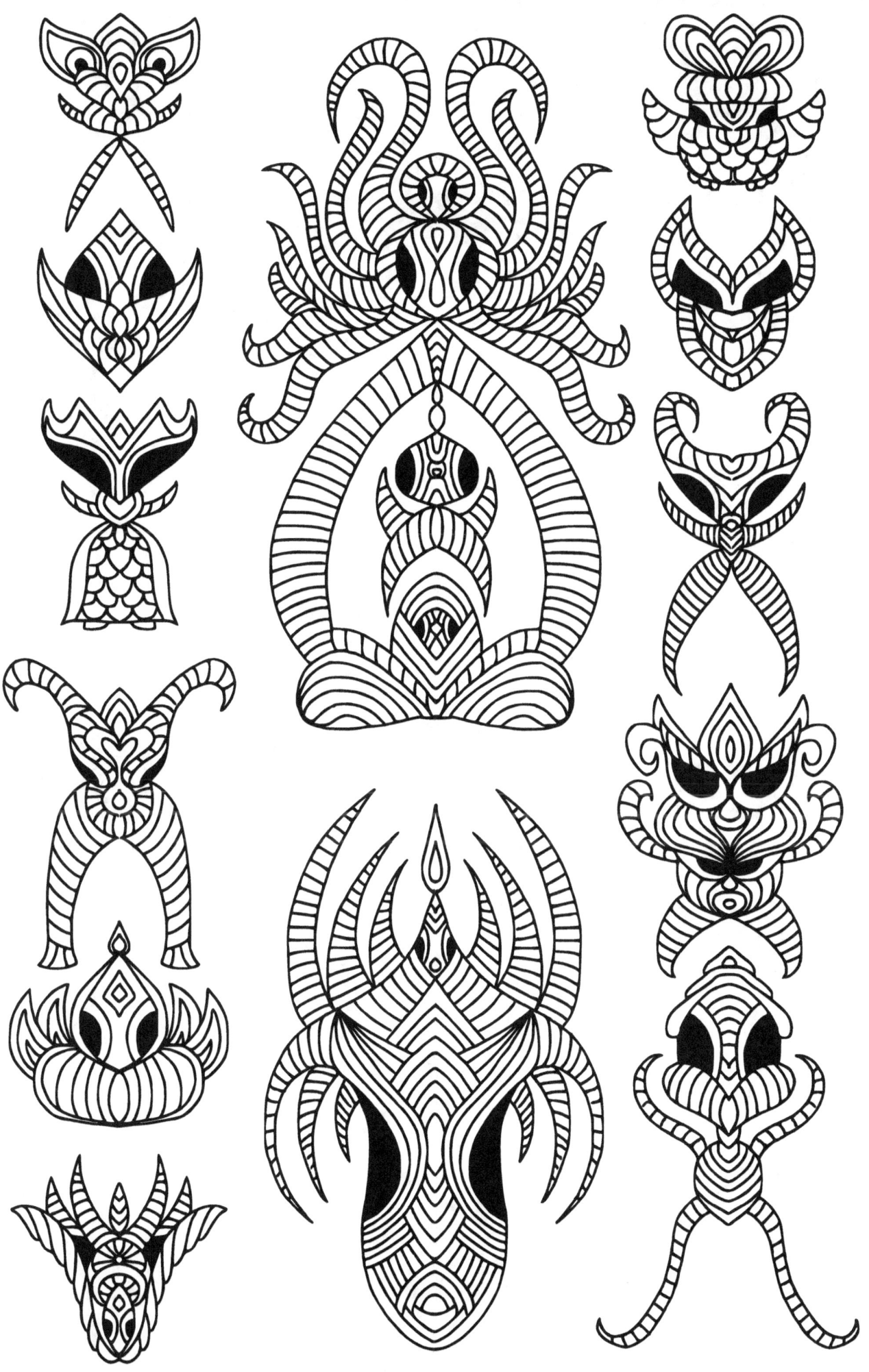

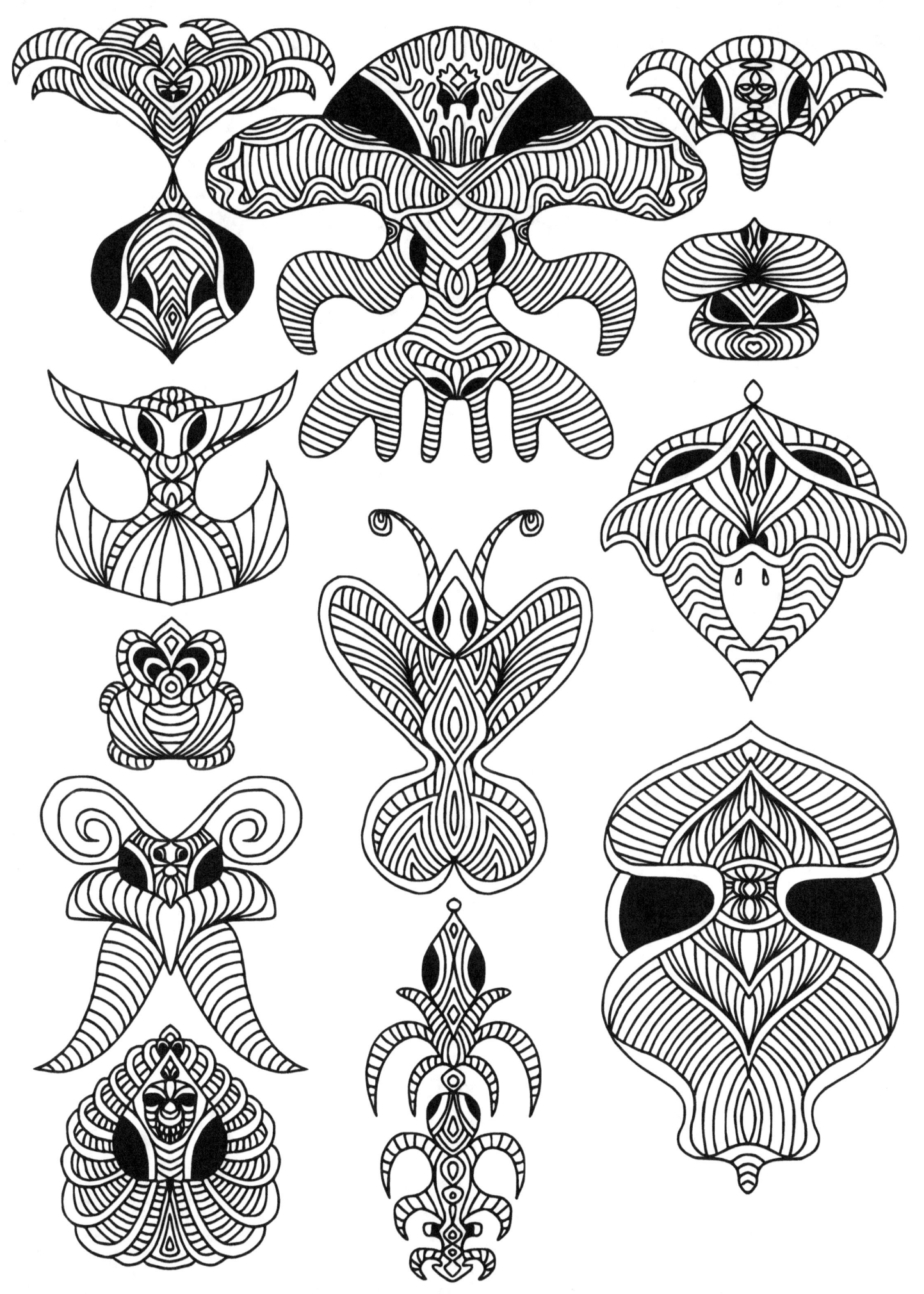

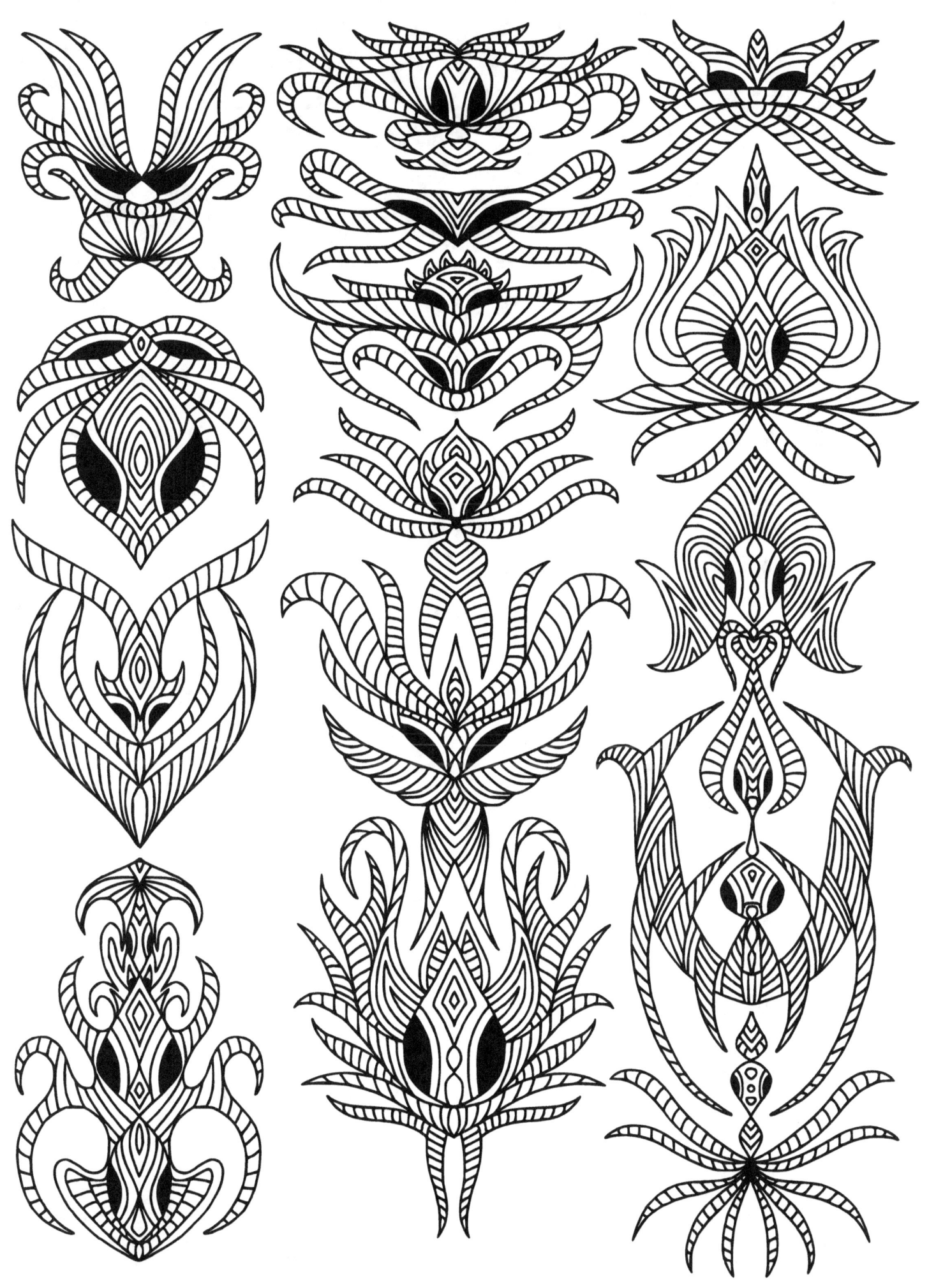

Test your colors here on the samples from
"My Pocket Coloring Companion"
&
"My Coloring Companion"

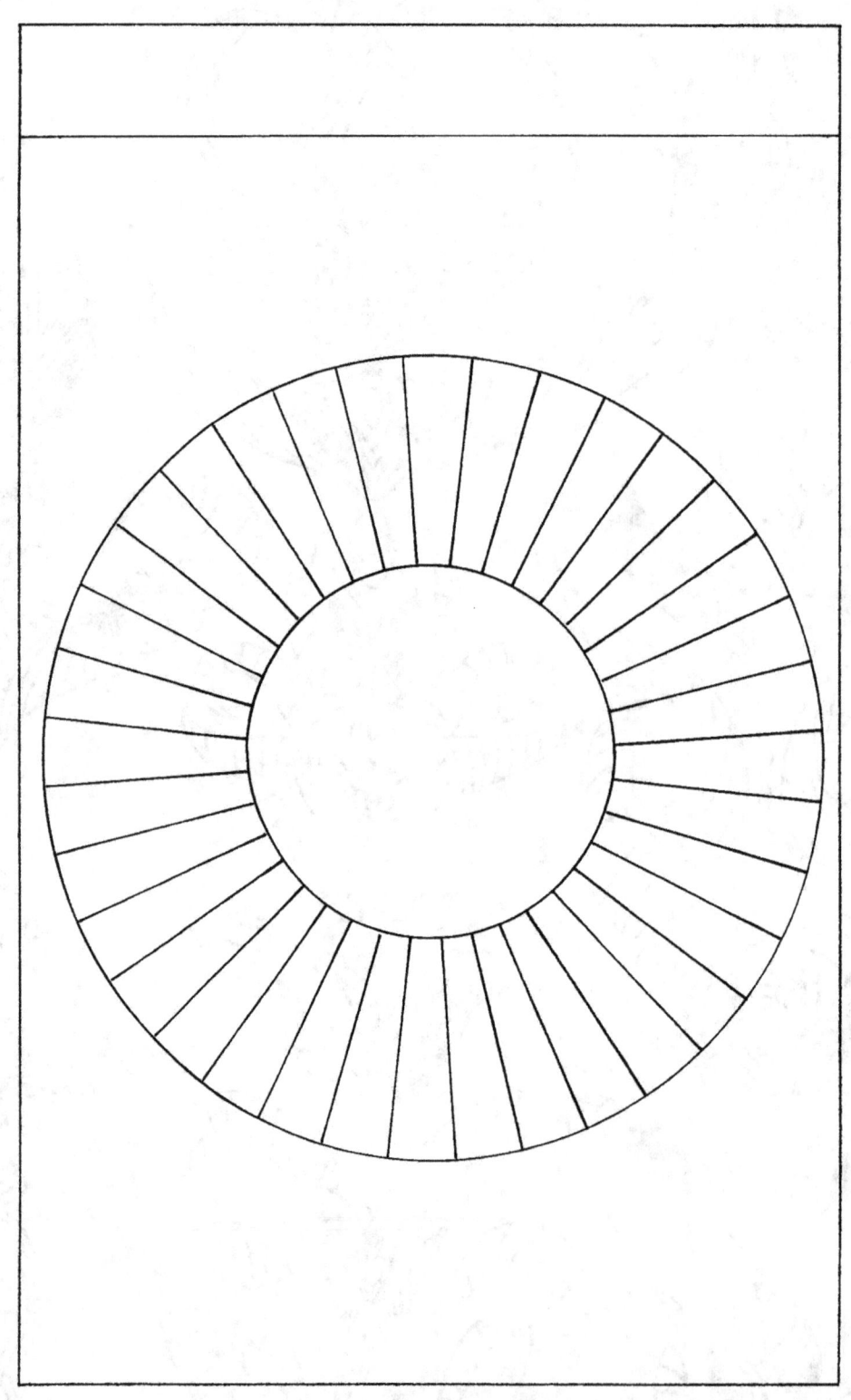

www.ingramcontent.com/pod-product-compliance
Lightning Source LLC
Chambersburg PA
CBHW082326220526
45470CB00008B/2416